OXFORD SPELLING

Dr Tessa Daffern

STUDENT BOOK

1

Name:

_____

Class:

_____

OXFORD
UNIVERSITY PRESS
AUSTRALIA & NEW ZEALAND

Oxford University Press is a department of the University of Oxford.
It furthers the University's objective of excellence in research,
scholarship, and education by publishing worldwide. Oxford is a registered
trademark of Oxford University Press in the UK and in certain other
countries.

Published in Australia by
Oxford University Press
Level 8, 737 Bourke Street, Docklands, Victoria 3008, Australia.

ISBN 9780190326098

Reproduction and communication for educational purposes
The Australian *Copyright Act 1968* (the Act) allows educational institutions that
are covered by remuneration arrangements with Copyright Agency to reproduce
and communicate certain material for educational purposes. For more information,
see copyright.com.au.

Edited by Laura Rentsch
Cover illustration by Lisa Hunt
Illustrated by Emma Trithart
Typeset by Integra Software Services Pvt. Ltd., Pondicherry, India
Proofread by Anita Mullick
Printed in China by Leo Paper Products Ltd

Acknowledgements
The author and the publisher wish to thank the following copyright holders for reproduction of their material.

All About Light by Julie Haydon, Oxford Reading for Comprehension, Oxford University Press, 2019; *Amazing National
Parks* by Janine Scott, Oxford Reading for Comprehension, Oxford University Press, 2019; *Amy & Louis* by Libby
Gleeson and Freya Blackwood, Text copyright © Libby Gleeson, 2006, Illustrations copyright © Freya Blackwood,
2006, First published by Scholastic Australia Pty Limited, 2006, Reproduced by permission of Scholastic Australia
Pty Limited; *Australian Spiders* by Carmel Reilly, Oxford Reading for Comprehension, Oxford University Press,
2018; *Don't Think About Purple Elephants* by Susan Whelan and Gwynneth Jones, Exisle Publishing; *Endangered
Australian Animals* by Carmel Reilly, Oxford Reading for Comprehension, Oxford University Press, 2019; *Flood* by
Jackie French and Bruce Whatley, Text copyright © Jackie French, 2011, Illustrations copyright © Bruce Whatley,
2011, First published by Scholastic Press, an imprint of Scholastic Australia, 2011, Reproduced by permission of
Scholastic Australia Pty Limited; *From Sand to Sea* by Cameron Macintosh, Oxford Reading for Comprehension,
Oxford University Press 2019; *Mr McGee and the Biting Flea* by Pamela Allen, Picture Puffin, 1999, Reproduced by
permission of Penguin Australia; *Save Our Water* by Julie Haydon, Oxford Reading for Comprehension, Oxford
University Press, 2019; *Waste-free Lunches* by Janine Scott, Oxford Reading for Comprehension, Oxford University
Press, 2019; *Wombat Stew* by Marcia K. Vaughan and Pamela Lofts, Text copyright © Marcia Vaughan, 1984,
Illustrations copyright © Pamela Lofts, 1984, First published by Scholastic Press, a division of Scholastic Australia
Pty Limited, 1984, Reproduced by permission of Scholastic Australia Pty Limited

The 'Bringing it together' activities provided online are adapted with permission from Daffern, T. (2018). *The
components of spelling: Instruction and assessment for the linguistic inquirer.* Literacy Education Solutions Pty Limited.

Every effort has been made to trace the original source of copyright material contained in this book. The
publisher will be pleased to hear from copyright holders to rectify any errors or omissions.

WELCOME TO OXFORD SPELLING

Welcome to *Oxford Spelling* **Student Book 1**! This book contains 28 units that you will use across the year, and that will help you gain new spelling knowledge and skills.

You will notice that each unit is divided into three sections:

- **Phonology (green section)**
- Orthography (blue section)
- **Morphology (purple section).**

This has been done to guide you in the types of thinking you might use to answer the questions in each section.

Tip

- In the phonology sections, think about the sounds you can hear in words.
- In the orthography sections, think about the letter patterns that you know.
- In the morphology sections, think about the meaning of base words, prefixes and suffixes.

At the end of each unit, your teacher will work with you on a 'Bringing it together' activity. This is a chance to bring together all the things you are learning about spelling and apply them to new words!

Your teacher, along with the *Oxford Spelling* superheroes, will be giving you lots of helpful information as you work through this book. Look out for the tips in each unit for handy hints on how to answer questions.

Enjoy *Oxford Spelling*, and meet the two superheroes who will help you become super spellers – Sunny Seb and Eco Eve!

1 Say each word. Listen for the short vowel phoneme in each word. Write each word in the correct box below.

| ran | pet | sad | lot | yes |

| him | just | wish | shop | lunch |

Short /a/	Short /e/	Short /i/	Short /o/	Short /u/

Tip

Each syllable feels like a beat and it has a vowel phoneme.

Amazing National Parks
by Janine Scott

There are amazing national parks all over the world. A national park is a protected area of land or water.

2 Read the text above.

The words listed at the top of the next page are from the text above. Clap along with the syllables you can hear in each word. Then write the number of syllables next to each word.

OXFORD UNIVERSITY PRESS

| amazing ___ | national ___ | park ___ | over ___ |
| world ___ | area ___ | land ___ | water ___ |

1 These words have a **short /a/** vowel phoneme. Write each word twice.

OXFORD WORDLIST

look → say → cover → write → check

bad		
sat		

2 These words have a **short /e/** vowel phoneme. Write each word twice.

pet		
yes		

3 These words have a **short /i/** vowel phoneme. Write each word twice.

him		
wish		

4 These words have a **short /o/** vowel phoneme. Write each word twice.

lot		
shop		

5 These words have a **short /u/** vowel phoneme. Write each word twice.

just		
lunch		

Morphology

> Compound words are made when two or more words are joined together to make a new word. For example, 'sun' and 'shine' join to become 'sunshine'.
> **Tip**

1 Join the pairs of words together to make compound words.

Word	+	Word	Compound word
to		day	
sun		day	

> **Tip** Days of the week have an upper-case letter at the beginning.

2 Use these compound words to help you to write the missing word in each sentence.

today	Sunday

a They went to the shops last _____.

b We will go to the shops _____.

Now try this unit's 'Bringing it together' activity, which your teacher will give you.

UNIT 2

Tip

A voiced phoneme uses your voice, like the **/th/** phoneme in 'there'.

An unvoiced phoneme is made using your breath instead of your voice, like the **/th/** phoneme in 'thunder'.

1 Say each word. Circle each word with an unvoiced **/f/** phoneme. Draw a line under each word with a voiced **/v/** phoneme.

free	brave	fish	cliff	waves

never	fall	enough	every	very

2 Say each word. Circle each word with an unvoiced **/th/** phoneme. Draw a line under each word with a voiced **/th/** phoneme.

this	three	than	think

they	thank	there

Tip

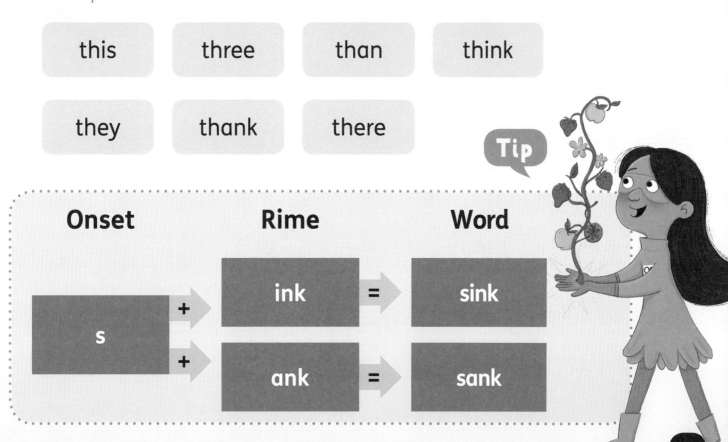

Onset	Rime	Word
s	ink	sink
	ank	sank

3 Use the onsets and the rimes to make words. Then say each word.

Onset	Rime	Word
s	ink	
w	ink	
p	ink	
t	ank	
b	ank	

1 Look for 'of' and 'off' in a book you are reading. Write a sentence from your book that has each word.

of _____

off _____

2 Choose from the words below to complete the sentences.

then	than	off	of

a   I have lost more teeth _____ my sister has.

b   I will take my socks _____.

OXFORD UNIVERSITY PRESS

c My friend ran down the hill and _____ ran back up the hill.

d We fed all _____ the fish in the fish tank.

3 Write each word twice.

look →→ say →→ cover →→ write →→ check

three		
than		
then		

Tip

Some words sound the same but look different and have a different meaning. These words are called homophones.

Morphology

1 The words below sound the same but have a different spelling and meaning.

    There   their   they're

Read the sentences below and write the missing homophones.

Flood
by Jackie French

- - - - - - - - - - - - - - - - - - - -

Boats tore from _____ jetties.

_____ were so many heroes now.

Some words can be joined together and then shortened. This is called a contraction. In a contraction, an apostrophe is used to replace one or more letters.

For example, 'they are' become joined and shortened to 'they're'. The letter **a** is replaced with an apostrophe.

2 Read this sentence:

> **They are going fishing.**

Write the sentence but change 'they are' to the contraction.

_____

3 Look for these homophones in a book you are reading. Write a sentence from your book that has each homophone.

there	
their	
they're	

Now try this unit's 'Bringing it together' activity, which your teacher will give you.

OXFORD UNIVERSITY PRESS

UNIT 3

1 Say each word. Listen for the vowel phoneme in each word. Write each word in the correct box below.

| cake | cat | eight | rain | hat |

Short /a/ phoneme	**Long /a/ phoneme**

1 Find the words in the word search.

c	a	k	e	z	n	h	g	d	f
z	b	f	g	j	a	s	t	a	y
b	p	l	a	y	d	m	l	y	o
t	v	a	g	d	g	r	e	a	t
a	w	a	y	o	h	r	m	g	d
t	s	i	o	n	a	m	e	g	q
a	r	e	e	v	w	o	w	a	y
k	b	h	m	a	k	e	e	m	t
e	s	y	a	r	z	q	t	e	m
o	m	y	n	q	y	m	a	t	e

great   game
ate   day
away   take
make   play
stay   name
way   cake

2 Write each word twice.

look → say → cover → write → check

game

take

cake

away

great

> **Tip**
>
> A split digraph is when two letters (such as **a-e**, **i-e** or **o-e**) work together to stand for one long vowel phoneme but are split by a consonant (as in 'm**a**k**e**', 'sl**i**d**e**' and 'r**o**p**e**').
>
> A quadgraph is when four letters stand for one speech sound (like **eigh** in the word 'eight').

3 Look at the different letter patterns that stand for **long /a/** vowel phonemes in a book you are reading. Write some words from your book on the correct lines to match the spelling of the **long /a/** vowel phonemes.

a-e _____

ai _____

ay _____

eigh _____

OXFORD UNIVERSITY PRESS

1 The words below sound the same but have a different spelling and meaning. They are homophones.

ate   eight

Write the missing homophones in the sentences below.

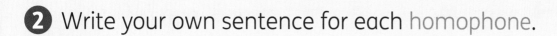

a   I _____ my lunch late.

b   The zoo has _____ apes.

c   Jin _____ _____ grapes.

2 Write your own sentence for each homophone.

ate	
eight	

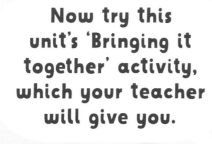

Now try this unit's 'Bringing it together' activity, which your teacher will give you.

UNIT 4

1 Say each word. Listen for the vowel phoneme in each word. Circle each word with a **long /e/** phoneme. Draw a line under each word with a **short /e/** phoneme.

sheep   nest   pen   bee

2 Look for some **short /e/** vowel phonemes and **long /e/** vowel phonemes in a book you are reading. Read the words out loud to help you. Write two words from your book in each box below.

Short /e/ phoneme	Long /e/ phoneme

From Sand to Sea
by Cameron Macintosh

A green turtle spends most of its life in the sea, but it starts its life on land.

3 Read the above sentence out loud.

Circle each word with a **long /e/** vowel phoneme.

OXFORD UNIVERSITY PRESS

Orthography

1 Write each word twice.

OXFORD WORDLIST: look → say → cover → write → check

tree		
sheep		
each		
beach		
weekend		

2 Look at the different letter patterns that stand for the **long /e/** vowel phoneme in a book you are reading. Write some words from your book on the correct lines to match the spelling of the **long /e/** vowel phoneme.

ee ______________________ ***ea*** ______________________

e ______________________

Morphology

1 Read each word below. Draw lines to match the pairs of homophones.

sea	bean	meat	be
bee	been	see	meet

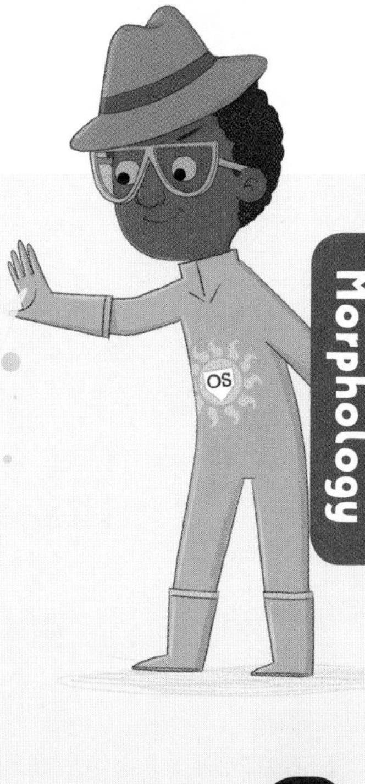

2 Write the missing homophones in the sentences below. Use a dictionary if you are not sure which homophone to use.

| be | bee | | meet | meat |

a I want to _____ a pilot when I grow up.

b Sometimes I have _____ in my sandwiches.

c Let's _____ Maya at the playground.

d The buzzing _____ was making honey.

3 Write your own sentence for each homophone.

sea	
see	
been	
bean	

Now try this unit's 'Bringing it together' activity, which your teacher will give you.

14

UNIT 5

1 Say each word. Listen for the vowel phoneme in each word. Write each word in the correct box below.

| boat | nose | frog | clock |

Short /o/ phoneme	**Long /o/ phoneme**

1 Find the words in the word search.

j	y	t	m	j	o	r	j	t	g
u	w	o	b	o	a	t	a	r	r
g	r	a	p	d	m	x	x	b	o
x	u	s	u	s	t	o	n	e	w
m	o	t	g	f	l	o	a	t	g
s	a	t	y	z	o	s	v	k	o
h	l	u	a	l	o	n	e	s	n
o	v	d	q	u	t	x	f	g	h
w	y	v	t	h	r	o	a	t	c
p	h	h	o	m	e	w	o	k	e

home   boat
woke   stone
show   float
toast   grow
alone   throat

2 Write each word twice.

look → say → cover → write → check

home		
woke		
show		

Write two more words with the **long /o/** vowel phoneme (as in 'boat').

3 Look at the different letter patterns that stand for **long /o/** vowel phonemes in a book you are reading. Write some words from your book into the correct boxes to match the spelling of the **long /o/** vowel phonemes.

oa as in 'boat'	**ow** as in 'show'	**o-e** as in 'home'	**o** as in 'go'

1 The words below sound the same but have a different spelling and meaning. They are homophones.

> no   know

Write the missing homophones in the sentences below.

a There were _____ boats left in the bay.

b We do not _____ how many stones are in the pond.

2 Write the missing word in each sentence by using the correct homophone.

> no   know   see   sea
>
> meet   meat   ate   eight

a Fish live in the _____.

b We will _____ at the bus stop after school.

c Antonio _____ all of the hot chips.

d Did you _____ that tadpoles are baby frogs?

A suffix is a letter or group of letters added to the end of a word to make a new word.

Tip

When the suffix **-ing** is added to the end of a word, it can tell us when something is happening.

3 Copy the base word on each line below. Then add the suffix **-ing** to make a new word.

row _____   blow _____

flow _____   grow _____

follow _____

4 Use the base word to help you to write the missing word in each sentence. Make sure that you add the suffix **-ing**.

> If the base word ends in *ow*, just add the suffix *-ing*.

row	We are _____ the boat.
blow	They are _____ up the balloons.
flow	The water in the river is _____ quickly.
grow	The plants are slowly _____ .
follow	The sheep are _____ one another.

Now try this unit's 'Bringing it together' activity, which your teacher will give you.

OXFORD UNIVERSITY PRESS

UNIT 6

1 Look at the pictures. What do you see? Say the word for each picture. Colour the pictures with the **long /oo/** phoneme (as in 'two') with a coloured pencil. Colour pictures with the **short /oo/** phoneme (as in 'took') with a lead pencil.

   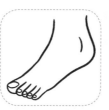  

2 Say each word. Listen for the vowel phoneme in each word. If you hear the **long /oo/** phoneme (as in 'food'), circle the word. If you hear the **short /oo/** phoneme (as in 'look'), draw a line under the word.

book	should	soon	put
broom	would	rude	flute

1 Find the words in the word search.

z	b	o	o	k	k	b	k	f	e
a	t	q	g	b	t	i	z	o	b
b	g	d	u	d	a	l	o	o	k
w	o	s	h	g	i	q	o	d	a
o	o	c	c	o	u	l	d	r	j
u	d	h	t	e	o	l	g	o	g
l	z	o	t	o	o	k	n	o	i
d	v	o	a	i	m	s	h	m	b
j	t	l	x	k	g	q	l	q	j
q	n	l	s	b	d	z	r	h	t

book   zoo

look   food

took   room

good   would

school   could

2 Write each word twice.

took		
good		
food		
room		
would		

3 Say each word. Listen for the vowel phoneme in each word. Look at the letter patterns that spell this vowel phoneme. Write the missing letter pattern on the line below. Then write two words in each box that matches its letter pattern. One is done for you.

moon	flew	threw	grew
room	broom	food	blew

Letter pattern: **oo**

moon

Letter pattern: _____

When the suffix **-ing** is added to a word, it can tell us that something is happening.

Many base words do not need to change before adding the suffix **-ing**.

1 Copy the base word on each line below. Then add the suffix **-ing** to make a new word.

look _____   cook _____

cool _____   scoop _____

swoop _____

2 In the boxes below, use each base word to write a sentence. Then write a new sentence that includes the base word with the suffix **-ing**. Use the example to help you.

look	I will **look** for birds in the trees.
	I am **looking** for birds in the trees.
cook	
swoop	
cool	

3 The words below sound the same but have a different spelling and meaning. They are homophones. Write the missing word in each sentence by using the correct homophone.

Tip

If you are not sure which homophone to use, look up the word in a dictionary and check the meaning.

to	too	two

wood	would	threw	through

a There were _____ birds in the

tree. They flew _____ the air.

b The apples fell _____ the ground.

c I _____ like to see the baboons at the zoo.

My brother would like to see the baboons _____.

d The table is made of _____.

e I _____ the ball as high as I could.

Now try this unit's 'Bringing it together' activity, which your teacher will give you.

OXFORD UNIVERSITY PRESS

UNIT 7

1 Look at the pictures. What do you see? Say the word for each picture. Colour the pictures with the **short /i/** phoneme (as in 'fish') with a lead pencil. Colour the pictures with the **long /i/** phoneme (as in 'ride') with a coloured pencil.

2 Say each word. Listen for the vowel phoneme in each word. Write each word in the correct box below.

| him | swing | cry | side | sky | miss |

| wide | drift | grip | night | wish | high |

Short /i/ phoneme	**Long /i/** phoneme

Rhyming words have the same ending sound.

Amy & Louis
by Libby Gleeson

Amy and Louis built towers as high as the sky.

3 Read the sentence above out loud. Circle the words that rhyme. Write the two rhyming words on the lines below.

_____   _____

1 Find the words in the word search.

y	o	i	x	q	v	z	g	c	r
s	w	q	x	n	t	x	z	c	p
l	l	q	z	i	t	b	t	w	r
i	i	g	w	c	y	u	r	l	i
d	k	b	l	e	t	u	y	e	n
e	e	b	b	t	i	c	n	x	c
d	l	g	i	o	m	r	b	x	e
b	g	x	u	g	e	p	e	i	s
l	k	v	z	f	u	u	p	f	s
s	h	u	p	b	y	y	m	d	h

by   time
try   slide
nice   princess
like

OXFORD UNIVERSITY PRESS

2 Write each word twice.

look ▸ say ▸ cover ▸ write ▸ check

by		
tried		
slide		
wish		
miss		

3 Say each word. Listen for the vowel phoneme in each word. Look at the letter patterns that spell this vowel phoneme. Write each word in the box that matches its letter pattern. One is done for you.

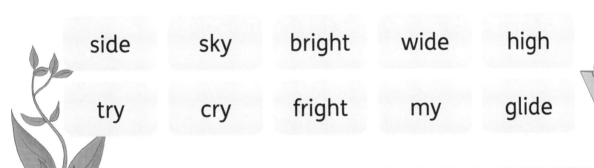

side   sky   bright   wide   high

try   cry   fright   my   glide

Letter pattern: *i-e*	Letter pattern: *igh*	Letter pattern: *y*
side		

1 Join the pairs of words together to make compound words.

Word	+	Word	Compound word
out		side	
in		side	

Use the compound words you have made to help you to write the missing word in each sentence.

a The stormy wind blew so we ran _____ the house.

b The day was bright and sunny so we went

_____ to play.

2 The words listed below are homophones. Write the missing word in each sentence using the correct homophone.

> **Tip**
> If you are not sure which homophone to use, look up the word in a dictionary and check the meaning.

| knight | night | by | bye | buy |

a We eat dinner at _____.

b He was standing _____ my side.

Now try this unit's 'Bringing it together' activity, which your teacher will give you.

OXFORD UNIVERSITY PRESS

1 For each onset, choose a rime that will make a word.
One is done for you.

Rimes	ing	ang	ong	ung

s__ong____   r_____   l_____   f_____

k_____   th_____   st_____   cl_____

br_____   sw_____

Mr McGee and the Biting Flea
by Pamela Allen

Mr McGee was running _____,

flying his kite and singing

a _____.

2 Choose from the words to complete the sentence above.

along   song

All About Light
by Julie Haydon

Light and heat are forms of energy.

3 Read the sentence above.

Count the number of phonemes you can hear in each word.
Write the number of phonemes under each word.

Words	light	and	heat	forms	of
Number of phonemes					

1 Find the words in the word search.

m	w	x	j	o	k	s	k	c	l	u	n	g	t	w
t	w	y	t	s	i	t	s	v	r	f	u	h	f	c
w	j	j	o	l	n	r	y	v	q	w	l	a	k	y
l	x	y	l	n	g	o	s	t	i	n	g	n	k	t
g	t	b	o	s	u	n	g	r	s	o	v	g	y	f
t	k	z	n	b	o	g	s	b	p	a	n	r	u	h
z	e	m	g	a	p	z	g	c	r	a	e	r	b	m
a	c	h	v	n	f	d	t	h	i	n	g	k	q	x
z	q	b	c	g	s	w	c	b	n	l	k	y	m	d
b	r	i	n	g	y	m	e	i	g	x	y	m	m	v

long
thing
king
hang
sting
strong
spring
lung
bring
bang
sung

2 Write each word twice.

look ➤ say ➤ cover ➤ write ➤ check

long		
thing		
king		

Tip

In some of the words listed below, the letters **ng** stand for one phoneme. Two letters that stand for one speech sound are called a digraph.

3 Write **n** or **ng** on each line below to make words. Then write each word in the correct box below.

pla_____

bri_____

i_____

gri_____

ri_____

stro_____

Words that end with **n**	Words that end with **ng**

A **contraction** is a shortened form of two words joined together. An apostrophe is used to replace one or more letters.

Tip

1 Look at the words in the table. Draw a line under the letters in the words that are replaced by the apostrophe.

Circle the apostrophes in the contractions.

Word	+	Word	Contraction
they		are	they're
did		not	didn't
do		not	don't
it		is	it's
I		am	I'm

2 Use the contractions from the table to fill in the missing words in these sentences. The first one is done for you.

_____I'm_____ feeling hungry.

a I _____ want to eat the string beans later.

b Today _____ all running late for school.

c Yesterday, it _____ rain. Now _____ raining.

Now try this unit's 'Bringing it together' activity, which your teacher will give you.

UNIT 9

1 For each onset, choose a rime that will make a word.
One is done for you.

Rimes	ock	ick	ack	eck	uck

s_ock_____   r_____   b_____

ch_____   sh_____   th_____

kn_____   wr_____   bl_____

cl_____   st_____   sn_____

2 Say each word out loud. Count the number of phonemes you can
hear in each word. Write each word in the correct box below.

black   sock   thick   neck

rock   trick   duck   flock

Words with three phonemes	Words with four phonemes

Look at the words that you have just written. Circle the letters
that make a digraph.

Draw a line under the letters that stand for a consonant blend.

1 Say each word. Listen for the **/k/** phoneme in each word. Look at the different letter patterns that can spell the **/k/** phoneme. Write a word in each box below.

clip	kite	echo	coin	sky	trick	black	school

c	k	ck	ch

2 Find the words in the word search.

a	s	q	s	o	t	r	i	c	k	h	e	c	b	c
j	t	t	h	i	c	k	c	j	a	g	s	a	l	c
x	u	c	l	o	c	k	o	u	s	f	a	r	a	u
q	c	h	k	e	v	a	m	w	r	e	c	k	c	t
x	k	x	g	z	t	z	e	p	v	m	h	u	k	e

car   black
come   trick
cute   clock
thick   wreck
           stuck

3 Write each word twice.

look → say → cover → write → check

car		
come		
cute		
black		

OXFORD UNIVERSITY PRESS

Add two more words that end with the **ck** digraph. Write each word two more times.

1 Read the words in the boxes below. Write the contractions next to the words.

Word	+	Word	Contraction
they		are	
it		is	
I		am	

2 Look for these contractions in a book you are reading. Write a sentence from your book that has each contraction.

didn't	
don't	

Now try this unit's 'Bringing it together' activity, which your teacher will give you.

UNIT 10

1 For each onset, choose a rime that will make a word. One is done for you.

Rimes	*itch*	*atch*	*etch*

c<u>atch</u>_____   f_____   l_____

h_____   st_____   tw_____

p_____   sn_____   sk_____

str_____   scr_____

> **Tip**
>
> A trigraph is three letters that represent one speech sound. An example is **tch**. These three letters stand for the **/ch/** phoneme in some words.

Look at the words that you have written on the lines above. Circle the trigraphs. Then draw a line under the consonant blends.

2 Read the words that you have written on the lines above. Count the number of phonemes you can hear in each word. Write two words in each box below.

Two words with three phonemes	Two words with four phonemes	Two words with five phonemes

OXFORD UNIVERSITY PRESS

The trigraph **tch** never appears at the start of a word but the digraph **ch** can appear at the start of a word.

1 Find the words in the word search.

e	c	r	s	c	r	a	t	c	h
s	h	w	a	t	c	h	g	a	s
v	i	k	j	m	u	c	h	p	w
m	p	s	t	r	e	t	c	h	i
u	s	c	i	s	j	f	k	v	t
e	a	c	h	c	w	q	s	u	c
h	y	c	h	i	c	k	e	n	h
w	n	g	v	c	h	e	e	s	e
d	l	d	a	q	w	s	h	e	a
p	m	m	a	t	c	h	i	r	i

much   match
chips   scratch
each   stretch
cheese   watch
chicken   switch

2 Write each word twice.

⭐ OXFORD WORDLIST   look ▸ say ▸ cover ▸ write ▸ check

chips	
each	
cheese	
chicken	
watch	

Add two of your own words that end with the **tch** trigraph.
Write each word two more times.

3 Say each word. Listen for the **/ch/** phoneme. Look at the different letter patterns that can spell the **/ch/** phoneme. Circle the words with **ch**. Draw a line under the words with **tch**.

munch	match	switch	chop
stretch	crunch	pitch	teach

A morpheme is the smallest unit of meaning. **Tip**

The word 'watched' has two morphemes, **watch** (the base word) and **-ed** (the suffix).

The suffix **-ed** is a morpheme that tells us that something has happened in the past.

1 Copy the base word on each line below. Then add the suffix **-ed** to make a new word.

watch _____   match _____

reach _____   peek _____

jump _____

OXFORD UNIVERSITY PRESS

2 In the boxes below, use the base word to write a sentence. Then write a new sentence that includes the base word with the suffix **-ed**. Use the example to help you.

watch	The dog will **watch** the sheep.
	The dog **watched** the sheep.
reach	

3 Look for some words with the suffix **-ed** in a book you are reading. Write a sentence from your book that has the suffix **-ed**. Then circle the word with the suffix **-ed**.

_____

_____

_____

_____

Now try this unit's 'Bringing it together' activity, which your teacher will give you.

1 For each onset, choose a rime that will make a word.

Rimes	edge	udge	idge

h_____   l_____   n_____

br_____   fr_____   pl_____

Tip

A trigraph is three letters that represent one speech sound. An example is **dge**. A digraph is two letters that represent one speech sound. An example is **ll**.

Write the words in the table below.

Words that end with **edge**	Words that end with **udge**	Words that end with **idge**

Look at the words that you have written in the boxes above. Circle the trigraphs. Draw a line under the consonant blends.

2 For each onset, choose a rime that will make a word.

Rimes	*ill*, as in 'hill'	*ell*, as in 'fell'	*all* or *awl*, as in 'call' or 'crawl'

ch_____   sh_____   st_____

sp_____   sm_____   sk_____

Look at the words that you have written on the lines above. Circle the digraphs. Draw a line under the consonant blends.

1 Write each word twice.

look → say → cover → write → check

cool		
old		
ball		
small		

Orthography

2 Say each word. Listen for the **/j/** phoneme in each word. Look at the different letter patterns that can spell the **/j/** phoneme. Notice that the letter patterns for the **/j/** phoneme in these words are **j**, **dge** and **ge**. Circle the letter pattern in each word that stands for the **/j/** phoneme.

jug	edge	age	cage	fridge	jog
job	bridge	rage	ridge	jam	grudge
wage	page	hedge	jet	just	wedge
sage	badge	joke	stage	jump	huge

Morphology

If the base word has a short vowel followed by one consonant letter, double the last letter and add the suffix -ed . **hop – hop**ped

1 Copy these words. Double the last letter and use the suffix **-ed** to make new words. Notice that the words are now about things that happened in the past.

hop _____   trip _____   tap _____

If the base word ends with x or with a consonant blend, digraph or trigraph, just add the suffix -ed.

bump – bumped   **crash – crash**ed   **scratch – scratch**ed

2 Copy these words. Use the suffix **-ed** to make new words.

jump _____   crash _____   melt _____

Tip

A medial vowel is the middle vowel phoneme in a word.

> If the base word has a medial vowel digraph, just add the suffix -ed.   **beep – beep**ed

3 Copy these words. Use the suffix **-ed** to make new words.

cool _____   float _____   need _____

> If the base word ends in e, drop the e and then add the suffix -ed.   **stumble – stumbl**ed

4 Drop the final **e** and add the suffix **-ed** to make new words.

grumble _____   tumble _____   battle _____

> If the base word ends in a consonant and then y, change the y to i and add the suffix -ed.   **carry – carr**ied

5 Change the final **y** to an **i** and use the suffix **-ed** to make new words.

carry _____   marry _____   ferry _____

Now try this unit's 'Bringing it together' activity, which your teacher will give you.

UNIT 12

Phonology

1 Say each word. Circle each word with an unvoiced **/f/** phoneme. Draw a line under each word with a voiced **/v/** phoneme.

| fish | of | fist | love | flash | vest | if | van |

| event | flick | live | friend | give | off | drive | life | save |

2 Using the words in the last activity, count the number of phonemes you can hear in each word. Write a word in each box below.

Two phonemes	Three phonemes	Four phonemes	Five phonemes

Orthography

1 Write each word twice.

look → say → cover → write → check

fish		
first		
live		
even		
every		

42

OXFORD UNIVERSITY PRESS

> **If a word ends with a /v/ phoneme, it is usually written as a digraph using the letters *ve*.**

2 Find the words in the word search.

x	i	f	b	t	h	i	n	k	m
w	l	j	l	z	m	o	n	u	m
v	k	p	o	i	k	e	v	e	n
b	v	v	v	i	t	j	f	j	e
l	f	o	e	y	h	w	i	r	k
i	i	v	o	t	a	j	s	f	j
v	r	r	j	q	n	b	h	v	h
e	s	p	s	e	v	e	r	y	b
d	t	x	w	d	t	h	i	s	l
o	f	f	t	h	r	e	e	y	o

this first
three if
think live
than love
off even
fish every

3 For each word listed below, write your own sentence.

than

then

1 The words 'for' and 'four' are homophones. Write the missing words in each sentence by using 'for' or 'four'.

a   My sister is _____ years old.

b   He waited _____ his friend to arrive.

c   They stayed at my house _____ _____ days.

Morphology

> **Tip**
>
> Words that show that there is more than one thing are called plural words.

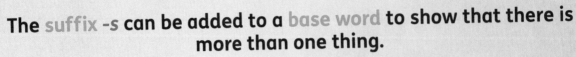

The suffix -s can be added to a base word to show that there is more than one thing.

But if a base word ends in s, x, z, ch or sh, add the suffix -es to show that there is more than one thing.

2 Write the missing word in each sentence to show that there is more than one. Use the base word to help you. Remember to check if you need to add **-es** or **-s** to the end of the base word.

Base word	Sentence
box	I put my toys in two _____.
brush	We have lots of _____ to paint a big picture.
bench	There are two _____ in the park.
glass	There were many _____ of juice to drink at the party.

Now try this unit's 'Bringing it together' activity, which your teacher will give you.

UNIT 13

> **Tip**
>
> A diphthong is a kind of long vowel sound that you make by moving your mouth in two ways. For example, **/ow/** in the word 'cow', and **/oi/** in the word 'boy'.

1 Say each word. Listen for the vowel sound in each word. Write each word under its vowel sound. One is done for you.

| down | toy | crown | joy | out |

| coin | proud | boy | house | join |

| brown | point | round | moist | soy |

/ow/ diphthong	**/oi/** diphthong
down	

1 Write each word twice.

look ▸ say ▸ cover ▸ write ▸ check

down		
about		
cow		
found		
around		

2 Think about the **/ow/** diphthong (as in 'cow').

Say each word. Listen for the **/ow/** diphthong in each word. Look at the different letter patterns that can spell the **/ow/** diphthong. Circle the words with **ow**. Draw a line under the words with **ou**.

how   shout   brown   now   house   town

mouse   crown   sound   frown   ground

OXFORD UNIVERSITY PRESS

If a base word ends with *s, x, z, ch* or *sh*, it is common to add the *-es* suffix to show that there is more than one thing.

1 Write the missing word in each sentence to show that there is more than one. Use the base word to help you.

box	Six _____ are full of toys.
dish	The kitchen sink was full of dirty _____.
beach	There are many _____ in the coastal town.
bus	Most of the _____ will arrive on time.

2 Make a compound word using the two words below.

| play | ground | |

Write a sentence that uses this compound word.

_____

_____

_____

Now try this unit's 'Bringing it together' activity, which your teacher will give you.

Phonology

1 Look at the pictures. What do you see? Say the word for each picture. Can you hear the **/w/** phoneme? Colour the pictures with the **/w/** phoneme.

> **Tip**
>
> Alliteration is a group of words that all include the same consonant phoneme, usually at the beginning of each word.
>
> For example: **big black bugs bounce**

2 Read the example of alliteration below. Listen for the repeating consonant phoneme. Then circle the letters in the words that stand for the repeating consonant phoneme.

Peter Piper picked a peck of pickled peppers.

3 Use the words below to write a sentence with alliteration.

wind   wail   why   when   wild   wet   won

will   walk   went   west   whale   whiz

_____

_____

_____

OXFORD UNIVERSITY PRESS

1 Write each word twice.

look ⋯▶ say ⋯▶ cover ⋯▶ write ⋯▶ check

well		
walk		
woke		
watch		
why		

2 Look for the **/w/** phoneme in a book you are reading. Look at the different letter patterns that can spell the **/w/** phoneme. Write some words with the **/w/** phoneme from your book into each box below.

Letter pattern: **w**	Letter pattern: **wh**

1 Read the sentences below and circle the homophones.

One apple cake is left. The baker of the apple cake won a prize.

2 The sentences below are based on two stories. Use the base words to help you write the missing plural words on the lines below, to show that there is more than one thing.

Don't Think about Purple Elephants
by Susan Whelan

Sophie closed her _____.
(eye)

Sophie smiled at funny _____.
(thing)

> If there is a *y* at the end of a base word, you often need to change it to *i* before you add the plural suffix.

Wombat Stew
by Marcia Vaughan

To make wombat stew, Dingo needs big blobs of mud, a few

emu feathers, one hundred _____, some
(fly)

slugs and bugs and creepy _____, and
(crawly)

lots of crunchy gum nuts.

Now try this unit's 'Bringing it together' activity, which your teacher will give you.

UNIT 15

1 Say each word. Listen for the vowel phoneme in each word. Circle each word with **/er/** (as in 'her'). Draw a line under each word with **/ar/** (as in 'far').

| first | dart | girl | park | herb |

| dirt | party | world | start | chart |

Endangered Australian Animals
by Carmel Reilly

Endangered animals are animals that are in danger of dying out. Animals can become endangered because of threats from:

- hunting
- changes to their habitat
- pollution.

2 Read the text above. Clap along with the syllables you can hear in each word. Then write two words in each box below.

Two words with one syllable	Two words with two syllables	Two words with three syllables

1 Write each word twice.

girl		
world		
another		
started		
farm		

2 Say each word. Listen to the vowel phoneme that comes before the **/r/** phoneme. Notice how the **/r/** phoneme changes the vowel phoneme. Then look at the letter patterns that stand for the **/er/** phoneme in each word. Circle the letter pattern that stands for the **/er/** phoneme in each word.

bird	turn	term	curl	first
mermaid	burn	germ	stir	curve
third	serve	herb	girl	disturb

> **Tip**
>
> When the suffix **-er** is added to the end of a base word, it can change the meaning of a word from an action (verb) to a person who does the action (noun). For example, 'farm' becomes 'farmer'.

> If the base word **ends in** e, **drop the** e **and add the** suffix **-er to change it to a person** noun.   *write – writer*

1 For each base word in the table, add the suffix **-er**. Then finish the sentences. Use the example to help you.

Base word	Base word + suffix **-er**	Sentence
teach	teacher	Mrs Patel teaches drawing. She is my art **teacher**.
bake		Angelo works at a bakery. He is a _____ .
drive		A person who drives a bus is a bus _____ .

2 Add **day** to the words below to make new compound words.

birth _____   week _____

some _____   every _____

> Now try this unit's 'Bringing it together' activity, which your teacher will give you.

1 These words have the **ear** trigraph. This **ear** trigraph can stand for different vowel phonemes. Draw a line to match the words with the same phoneme.

earth	bear
clear	learn
pear	hear

Save Our Water
by Julie Haydon

People must conserve water by using less of it. We can conserve water by turning off taps and having shorter showers.

2 Read the text above. Clap along with the syllables you can hear in each word. Then write three words in each box below.

Three words with one syllable	Three words with two syllables

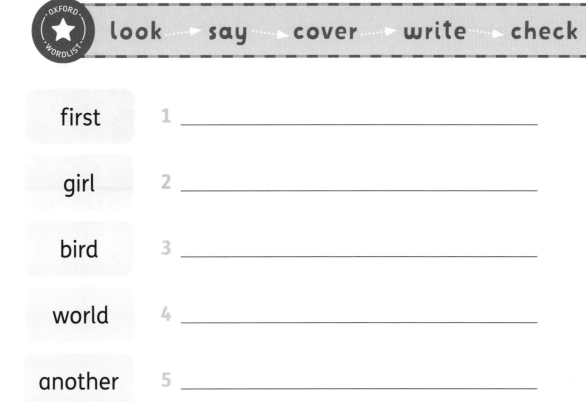

1 Write these words in alphabetical order.

look → say → cover → write → check

first	1	_____
girl	2	_____
bird	3	_____
world	4	_____
another	5	_____
park	6	_____
party	7	_____
started	8	_____
farm	9	_____

2 Use at least three words from the list above to write your own sentence. Circle each word in your sentence that came from the list.

_____

_____

_____

3 Say each word. Listen for the diphthong in each word. Look at the different letter patterns that can spell the diphthong. Write each word in the correct box below. One is done for you.

boy	moist	coin	toy
point	soy	spoil	enjoy

Letter pattern: **oy**

boy

Letter pattern: **oi**

Morphology

Tip

The suffix **-er** can be added to a word to compare things.

For example, this sentence compares two mountains.

This mountain is high but that mountain is higher.

1 Read the rules and the examples in the tables on the next page. Use them to help you add the suffix **-er** to the base words.

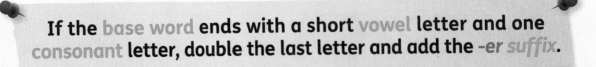

If the base word ends with a short vowel letter and one consonant letter, double the last letter and add the -er suffix.

OXFORD UNIVERSITY PRESS

big	*bigger*	The red box is **bigger** than the black box.
thin		Paper is _____ than cardboard.

 If the base word **ends in e, drop the e and add the** suffix -er.

large	*larger*	Birds are **larger** than butterflies.
brave		Now I am older and _____.

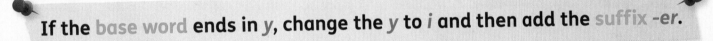 **If the** base word **ends in y, change the y to i and then add the** suffix -er.

happy	*happier*	I feel **happier** when I am with my friends than on my own.
silly		Clowns are _____ than pirates.

 If the base word **ends with a** consonant digraph, trigraph **or** blend, **or if it has a medial** vowel digraph, **just add the** suffix -er .

long	*longer*	The snake is **longer** than the worm.
sweet		Strawberries are _____ than limes.

Now try this unit's 'Bringing it together' activity, which your teacher will give you.

1 Say each word. Listen for the vowel phoneme.
Write each word in the correct box below.

| bad | game | crab | play |

| brain | than | chat |

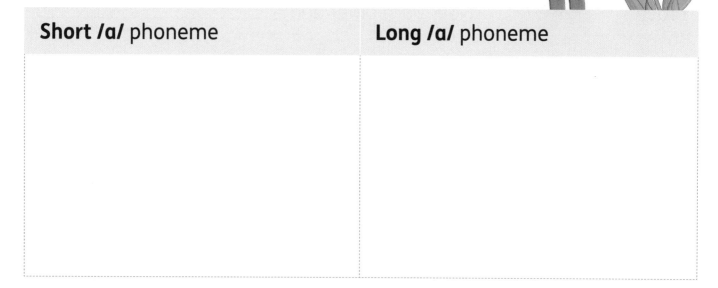

Short /a/ phoneme	Long /a/ phoneme

2 Read out loud from a book you are reading. Write five words
from your book that have a **short /a/** vowel phoneme. Then write
five words from your book that have a **long /a/** vowel phoneme.

Short /a/ phoneme	Long /a/ phoneme

1 Say each word. On the lines below, write the missing letter patterns that spell the **long /a/** vowel phoneme in each word. Then write each word in the box that matches its letter pattern. One is done for you.

play	rain	frame	eight	stay
paint	gate	weigh	pay	chain
shake	drain	neigh	spray	weight

Letter pattern: **ay**

play

Letter pattern: _____

Letter pattern: _____

Letter pattern: _____

② Write these words in alphabetical order.

look ▶ say ▶ cover ▶ write ▶ check

game   make   take   cake   play   holiday

1 _____   2 _____

3 _____   4 _____

5 _____   6 _____

Morphology

① Write the missing homophones in the sentences below. Use a dictionary if you are not sure which homophone to use.

ate   eight   new   knew

a We _____ the

_____ bunches of grapes.

b I _____ that the

_____ shoes would fit better.

Now try this unit's 'Bringing it together' activity, which your teacher will give you.

OXFORD UNIVERSITY PRESS

UNIT 18

1 Say each word. Circle each word with a **short /e/** phoneme.
Draw a line under each word with a **long /e/** phoneme.

set	sleep	dream	met	tree	let
sheep	get	left	egg	tea	sent
each	bent	beach	then	sheet	

2 Read out loud from a book you are reading. Write
five words from your book that have a **short**
/e/ vowel phoneme. Then write five words
from your book that have a **long /e/**
vowel phoneme.

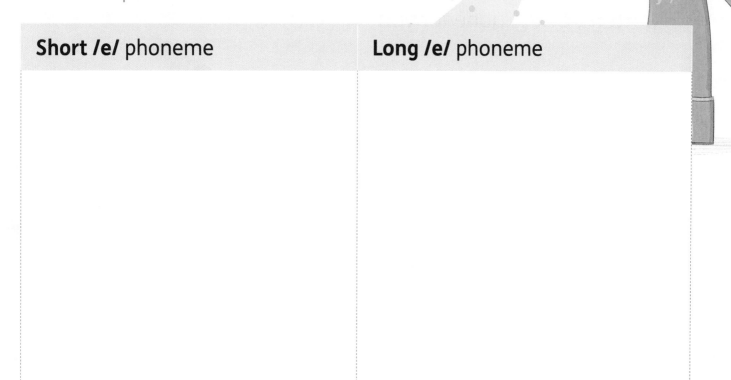

Short /e/ phoneme	**Long /e/** phoneme

1 Write these words in alphabetical order.

set

egg

sleep

tree

each

1 _____

2 _____

3 _____

4 _____

5 _____

2 Say each word out loud. Listen for the **long /e/** vowel phoneme in each word. Look at the letter patterns that spell this **long /e/** vowel phoneme. Write the missing letter patterns on the lines on the next page. Then write each word in the box that matches its letter pattern. One is done for you.

he   me   seed   sea

beast   speed   be   sweet

she   bead   pea   cheap

queen   clean

OXFORD UNIVERSITY PRESS

Letter pattern: *ea*	Letter pattern: _____	Letter pattern: _____
sea		

3 Write each word twice.

look → say → cover → write → check

tea			
sheep			
beach			

1 Write the missing homophones in the sentences on the next page. Use a dictionary if you are not sure which homophone to use.

see	sea	been	bean
meet	meat	be	bee

a We swam in the _____.

b I have _____ away for a week.

c Let's _____ at the park.

d I will _____ going to the library today.

Tip

Homographs are words with the same spelling but a different meaning and sometimes a different sound.

2 Look at the words that are spelled the same in these sentences. These are homographs. Read each sentence out loud. Use the words on either side of the homographs to help you decide how to say them.

> **A *tear* ran down my face.**
>
> ***Tear* the paper in half.**

3 Read the sentences below. Circle the homograph in each sentence.

> **I will read a book tonight. I read a book last night.**

Now try this unit's 'Bringing it together' activity, which your teacher will give you.

OXFORD UNIVERSITY PRESS

UNIT 19

1 Say each word. Circle each word with a **short /o/** phoneme.
Draw a line under each word with a **long /o/** phoneme.

lot	boat	throat	shop	dog	foam

home	shot	float	block	grow	woke

clock	show	cross	moss	snow	frog

groan	unlock	postcode	drop

2 Read out loud from a book you are reading. Write
five words from your book that have a **short /o/**
vowel phoneme. Then write five words from
your book that have a **long /o/** vowel phoneme.

Short **/o/** phoneme	Long **/o/** phoneme

1 Say each word. On the lines below, write the missing letter patterns that stand for the **long /o/** vowel phoneme. Then write each word in the box that matches its letter pattern. One is done for you.

boat	bone	grow	home	flow	smoke
throat	snow	stone	toad	show	note
float	toast	know	groan	rose	window
coast	goat	yellow	phone	roast	froze
follow	close	elbow	spoke	soap	

Letter pattern: **oa**	Letter pattern: _____	Letter pattern: _____
boat		

OXFORD UNIVERSITY PRESS

2 Write each word twice.

dog		
home		
woke		
show		
snow		

1 The words listed below all end in the suffix *-er*.
Circle the words that are nouns (names) for the jobs that
people do. Then write each base word without the suffix.

teacher	
bigger	
painter	

louder	
writer	
happier	

**Now try
this unit's 'Bringing
it together' activity,
which your teacher
will give you.**

Morphology

UNIT 20

1 Say each word. Listen for the vowel phoneme in each word. There are four different vowel phonemes in these words. Write each word in the correct box below.

stop	should	chop	hope	hop	stood
home	rude	room	foot	bush	soap
soon	bone	chew	block		

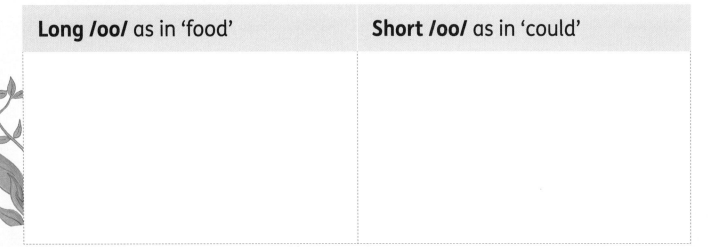

Short /o/ as in 'lot'	**Long /o/** as in 'boat'

Long /oo/ as in 'food'	**Short /oo/** as in 'could'

2 Circle the letters that stand for the vowel phoneme in each word you just wrote above.

OXFORD UNIVERSITY PRESS

1 Say each word. On the lines below, write the missing letter patterns that stand for the **long /oo/** vowel phoneme. Then write each word in the box that matches its letter pattern. One is done for you.

broom   flew   flute   glue   ute   true

new   blue   cute   blew   moon

stew   room   mute   soon

Letter pattern: **oo**

broom

Letter pattern: _____

Letter pattern: _____

Letter pattern: _____

2 Write each word twice.

look ⤳ say ⤳ cover ⤳ write ⤳ check

look		
school		
could		

3 Say each word. Look at the letter patterns that spell the **short /oo/** vowel phoneme. Circle each word with the letter pattern **oo**. Draw a line under each word with the letter pattern **oul**.

good   should   stood   would   book   could

Morphology

1 Write the missing homophones in the sentences below. Use a dictionary if you are not sure which homophone to use.

to   too   two   wood   would

a The _____ pizzas were _____

big for us _____ finish.

b I _____ like to buy the _____.

Now try this unit's 'Bringing it together' activity, which your teacher will give you.

UNIT 21

1 Say each word. Listen for the vowel phoneme. Write each word in the correct box below.

| by | miss | try | wish | nice |

| like | time | chicken | princess | chin |

Short /i/ phoneme	**Long /i/** phoneme

2 Read out loud from a book you are reading. Write three words from your book that have a **short /i/** vowel phoneme. Then write three words from your book that have a **long /i/** vowel phoneme.

Short /i/ phoneme	**Long /i/** phoneme

1 Say each word. On the lines below, write the missing letter patterns that stand for the **long /i/** vowel phoneme. Then write each word in the box that matches its letter pattern. One is done for you.

nice	sight	cry	right	slide	might
flight	glide	fly	bright	ride	try
delight	my	tight	size	sigh	dry
mobile	by	hide	write		

Letter pattern: **i-e**   Letter pattern: _____   Letter pattern: _____

nice

OXFORD UNIVERSITY PRESS

2 Write these words in alphabetical order.

look → say → cover → write → check

| by | tried | nice | like | time | princess |

1 _____   2 _____

3 _____   4 _____

5 _____   6 _____

1 Write the missing homophones in the sentences below. Use a dictionary if you are not sure which homophone to use.

| by | bye | buy |

a I will _____ some bread and milk.

b I said _____ to my teacher.

c We walked _____ the classroom.

| there | their | they're |

d The bikes are kept safely over _____.

e The red bikes are _____ bikes, not our bikes, but

_____ going to let us ride on the red bikes.

Now try this unit's 'Bringing it together' activity, which your teacher will give you.

Phonology

1 Each word below has two syllables. For some of these words, the first syllable is accented (the beat feels strong). For the other words, the second syllable is accented. Circle the words that have an accented first syllable.

bottle	little	believe	ripple	rabbit
rainbow	today	painter	mistake	prefer
behave	attack	crayon	remind	carry

Tip

A disyllabic word is a word with two syllables.

To help you work out which syllable is accented, clap the beats in each word. Notice that an accented syllable will have a stronger clap.

2 Listen to the sentence that your teacher reads. Listen for the alliteration that uses the **/kw/** blend. Circle the **/kw/** blend in each word.

The queasy queen quarrelled quietly with quolls.

3 Write your own sentence with alliteration using any of the words listed below. You may add suffixes to some of these words.

quack	quiet	quiver	quite
quick	quilt	queen	quail

_____

_____

_____

1 Write each word twice.

look ▸ say ▸ cover ▸ write ▸ check

people		
finally		
queen		

Tip

A schwa is a common vowel sound that is not long or short. Instead it makes an **/uh/** sound. It can be heard in an unaccented syllable, for example the **/al/** in 'final'.

2 Say each word. Clap along with the syllables in each word. Notice that each word ends with a schwa and an **/l/** consonant phoneme.

On the line below, write the missing letter pattern that spells this last sound. Then write each word in the box that matches its letter pattern. One is done for you.

| people | final | little | table | dial |
| trial | cycle | spiral | title | |

Letter pattern in last syllable: **le**	Letter pattern in last syllable: _____
people	

The suffix **-ly** can be added to a word to describe **Tip** *how* something is done. Words that describe how something is done are called adverbs.

1 Read the base words below. Then change each word to an adverb by adding the suffix **-ly**.

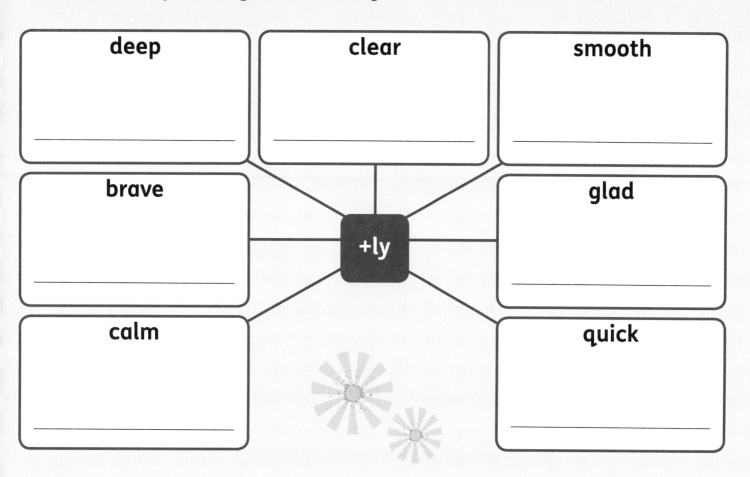

deep

_____

clear

_____

smooth

_____

brave

_____

glad

_____

+ly

calm

_____

quick

_____

2 Read each sentence below. Then choose from the adverbs above to add more detail to each sentence.

a   We _____ walked through the dark forest.

b   The train moved _____ along the tracks.

c   I _____ helped my little sister.

Now try this unit's 'Bringing it together' activity, which your teacher will give you.

Phonology

1 Write your own sentence with alliteration using any of the words listed below. You may add suffixes to some of these words.

| dry | dribble | drip | drop | drag | dragon |

| dress | drink | drank | drive | draw |

_____

_____

2 Listen to this sentence as your teacher reads. Listen for the alliteration that uses a consonant blend. Circle the letters that stand for the consonant blends. Then write the consonant blend.

Blair blogged blissfully about blue blossoms blooming.

Consonant blend: _____

Waste-free Lunches

by Janine Scott
- - - - - - - - - - - - - - - - - - - -

No packets, please! Supermarkets are full of food in packaging. Sultanas come in cardboard boxes. Chips come in foil bags. Muesli bars come in plastic wrappers.

3 Read the text above. Clap along with the syllables you can hear in each word. Then write one word in each box on the top of the next page.

Two syllables	Three syllables	Four syllables

1 Write each word twice.

look → say → cover → write → check

brother		
water		
other		
over		
ever		
baby		

2 Say each word. Clap along with the syllables in each word. On the lines below, write the missing letter patterns that spell the vowel phoneme in the last syllable. Then write each word in the box that matches its letter pattern. One is done for you.

danger	doctor	colour	water	harbour
actor	super	author	enter	mirror
anger	tractor	favour	better	brother
sailor	sister	flavour	other	
neighbour	clever	over		

Letter pattern in last syllable: **er**	Letter pattern in last syllable: _____	Letter pattern in last syllable: _____
danger		

OXFORD UNIVERSITY PRESS

1 The words listed below end in the suffix **-ly**. Write the base word on the line next to each word.

loudly _____ safely _____ kindly _____

slowly _____ suddenly _____

2 Use the **-ly** words listed above to write your own sentences. Start your sentences with **who**, then write **what** happens, and then write **how** it happens. Read the example in the table below. Notice that the last word in the sentence ends with the suffix **-ly**.

Who?	What?	How?
The people	talked	loudly.

Now try this unit's 'Bringing it together' activity, which your teacher will give you.

1 Write your own sentence with alliteration using any of the words listed below. You may add suffixes to some of these words.

green	grandma	grass	grow	grew
grab	grub	grape	grand	great

_____

_____

Draw a line under all the consonant blends in the words above.

Australian Spiders
by Carmel Reilly

There are about 2000 species of spiders in Australia.

All spiders are venomous … Only some spiders are harmful to humans.

2 Read the text above. Clap along with the syllables you can hear in each word. Write a word in each box below.

Two syllables	Three syllables	Four syllables

1 Write each word twice.

look ····▸ say ···· cover ····▸ write ···▸ check

grow		
rabbit		
soccer		
dinner		
bunny		

2 Choose two words that you are finding tricky to spell and write them three times.

Tip

If the first syllable of a disyllabic word (a word with two syllables) has a short vowel and one consonant, the consonant letter is usually doubled.

The rabbit has two long ears.

3 Say each word. Look at the letter patterns that spell the medial (middle) consonant phoneme in each word. Then write each word in the correct box below.

| rabbit | soccer | baby | dinner | silent | lady |

| human | little | happy | pirate | kitten | carrot |

| chosen | tennis | tidy | season |

Consonant is doubled	Consonant is *not* doubled

a   In the left column, draw a line under the letters that make a short vowel and consonant letter pattern in the middle of each word.

b   In the right column, circle the letters that make a long vowel and consonant letter pattern in the middle of each word.

OXFORD UNIVERSITY PRESS

The **suffix -s** can be added to a base word to show that there is more than one thing.

Tip

If a base word ends in **f** or **fe**, you usually change the **f** or **fe** to the letter **v** and then add the suffix **-es** to show that there is more than one thing.

1 Write the missing word in each sentence to show that there is more than one thing. Use the base word to help you. Remember to add the suffix **-es** to the end of the base word that you write. Read the example first.

Base word	Sentence
wolf	There are many wolves lurking in the forest.
shelf	The library has lots of _____ full of books.
knife	The table was set with plates, forks and _____.
leaf	In autumn, all of the _____ fall off the fruit trees.

Now try this unit's 'Bringing it together' activity, which your teacher will give you.

UNIT 25

1 Say each word. Draw a line under each consonant blend in these words.

| tree | train | treat | trap | truck | trip | tractor |

| tray | try | trust | true | trample | trail | trend |

2 Write your own sentence with alliteration using any of the words listed above. You may add suffixes to some of these words.

_____

_____

3 Look at the pictures below and write the missing letters in each word.

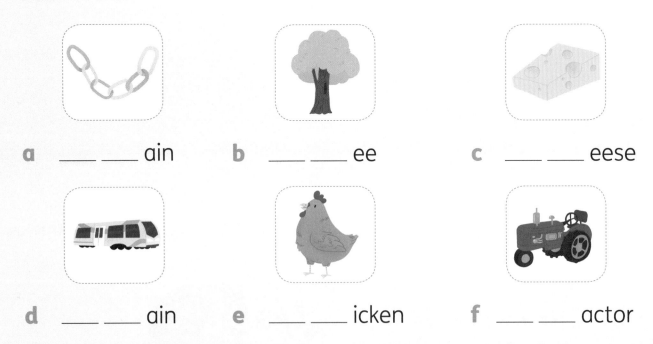

a ___ ___ ain   b ___ ___ ee   c ___ ___ eese

d ___ ___ ain   e ___ ___ icken   f ___ ___ actor

Look at the letters you wrote. Circle each consonant digraph **ch**. Draw a line under each consonant blend **tr**.

OXFORD UNIVERSITY PRESS

1 Say each word. On the line below, write the missing letter pattern that stands for diphthong **/ow/**. Then write each word in the box that matches its letter pattern. One is done for you.

spout	how	shower	now	tower
house	down	out	clown	shout
gown	bound	snout	town	count
sound	ground	power	allow	around

Letter pattern: *ou*

spout

Letter pattern: _____

2 Write each word twice.

look → say → cover → write → check

or		
more		
door		
morning		
forest		
tree		
train		

3 Choose two words that you are finding tricky to spell and write them three times.

OXFORD UNIVERSITY PRESS

1 Join the pairs of words together to make compound words.

Word	+	Word	Compound word
a		gain	
week		end	

Use the compound words to help you to finish the sentences.

I had fun at the beach last _____. I would

like to go _____.

2 Write the missing word in each sentence to show that there is more than one. Use the base word to help you.

Base word	Sentence
rabbit	There are many _____ hopping around.
peach	Lots of _____ are growing on the tree.
city	There are eight capital _____ in Australia.
kangaroo	The _____ are eating grass.

Now try this unit's 'Bringing it together' activity, which your teacher will give you.

UNIT 26

Phonology

1 Write your own sentence with alliteration using any of the words listed below. You may add suffixes to some of these words. Then draw a line under each consonant blend in these words.

crooked	cry	crunch	crisp	crop
cream	crab	crow	cross	crawl
crayon	crash	creek	crack	

_____

_____

2 Look at the pictures below and write the missing letters. Then circle each consonant blend **cr**. Draw a line under each blend **gr**. Draw a tick next to each blend **dr**.

a ___ ___ ab   b ___ ___ een   c ___ ___ apes

d ___ ___ um   e ___ ___ ayons   f ___ ___ agon

1 Write each word twice.

look → say → cover → write → check

crazy		
green		
grandma		
grass		
dragon		

2 Say each word. On the line below, write the missing letter pattern that stands for the diphthong. Then write each word in the box that matches its letter pattern. One is done for you.

toilet	point	destroy	toy
soy	spoil	enjoy	coin

Letter pattern: *oi*	Letter pattern: _____
toilet	

1 Use the base words to write words with suffixes in the tables below. Use the rules to help you.

When a base word ends with a short vowel phoneme followed by a single letter that stands for a consonant phoneme, double the last letter before adding the suffix *-ed* or *-ing*.

Base word	Add *-ed*	Add *-ing*
trip		

If a word ends with a long vowel phoneme followed by a consonant sound, it is usual to just add the suffix *-ed* or *-ing*. You don't need to change the base word.

Base word	Add *-ed*	Add *-ing*
float		

If a word ends with the letter *y*, just add the suffix *-ing*. Change the *y* into an *i* before you add the suffix *-ed*.

Base word	Add *-ed*	Add *-ing*
hurry		

OXFORD UNIVERSITY PRESS

2 Use the base words to write the missing words. Add a suffix where it is needed. Use the rules to help you.

> If a word ends with a consonant blend, it is usual to just add the suffix *-ed* or *-ing*. You don't need to change the base word.

jump

They will _____ over the rock.

They are _____ over the rock.

> If a word ends with the letter e, you need to drop the e before you add the suffix *-ed* or *-ing*.

wobble

The jelly was _____ on the plate.

The jelly _____ on the plate.

> If a word ends with a long vowel phoneme, it is usual to just add the suffix *-ed* or *-ing*. You don't need to change the base word.

show

The teacher _____ us where the library is.

The teacher is _____ us where the library is.

Now try this unit's 'Bringing it together' activity, which your teacher will give you.

Phonology

1 Say each word. Circle each consonant blend in the words.

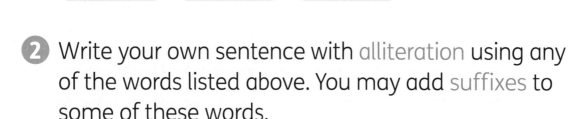

snake	snow	snail	snip
snoop	snug	snout	snack
snag	sneak	snap	

2 Write your own sentence with alliteration using any of the words listed above. You may add suffixes to some of these words.

_____

_____

_____

3 Look at the pictures below and write the missing letters in each word.

a ___ ___ ake   **b** ___ ___ out   **c** ___ ___ oke   **d** ___ ___ elly

Look at the letters you wrote. Circle each consonant blend **sn**. Draw a line under each consonant blend **sm**.

OXFORD UNIVERSITY PRESS

Tip

If a word ends with a **/v/** phoneme and has the letter **v**, it must be written as a digraph using the letters **ve**.

1 The words below end with the **/v/** phoneme. Use the tip to write the missing letter at the end of each word. Then write each word again. Say each word.

lov ____	
hav ___	
giv ___	

dov ___	
activ ___	
relativ __	

2 Write each word twice.

★ OXFORD WORDLIST

look ▸ say ▸ cover ▸ write ▸ check

snake		
love		
live		
even		
every		

3 Choose two words that you are finding tricky to spell and write them three times.

A prefix is a meaningful unit of letters that can be added to the start of a word to make a new word.

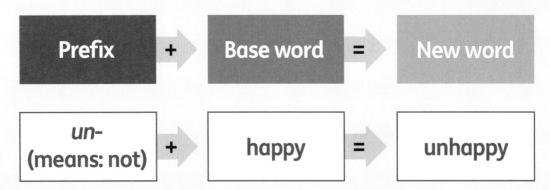

Prefix	+	Base word	=	New word
un- (means: not)	+	happy	=	unhappy

1 Change these words to their opposite meaning by writing the prefix **un-** before the base word. Then write each word again.

_____ do		_____ true	
_____ pack		_____ lucky	
_____ able		_____ safe	
_____ zip		_____ well	
_____ tie			

Now try this unit's 'Bringing it together' activity, which your teacher will give you.

96

OXFORD UNIVERSITY PRESS

OS

UNIT 28

1 Say each word. Draw a line under each consonant blend.

| spoil | spoon | speed | speak | spot |

| spray | spin | sport | spill | spice |

| sparkle | spy | spider | space |

2 Write your own sentence with alliteration using any of the words listed above. You may add suffixes to some of these words.

_____

_____

3 Look at the pictures and write the missing letters in each word. Then look at the letters you wrote. Circle each consonant blend **sp**. Draw a line under each consonant blend **st**.

a ___ ___ ider

b ___ ___ ar

c ___ ___ ick

d ___ ___ ots

e ___ ___ in

f ___ ___ orm

1 Write these words in alphabetical order.

OXFORD WORDLIST

look ▸ say ▸ cover ▸ write ▸ check

last   also

only   scared

who   cousin

castle   movie

spider

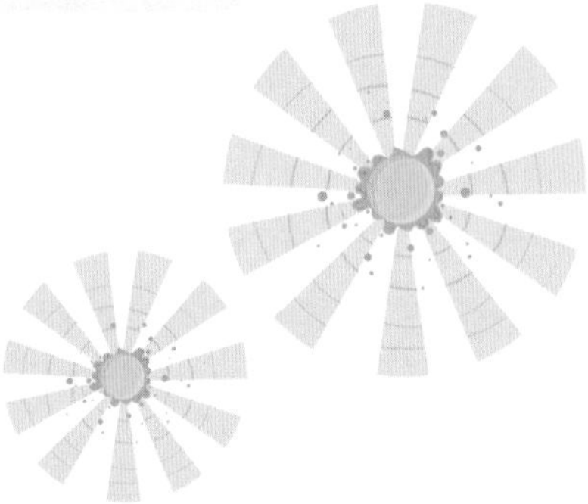

1 _____

2 _____

3 _____

4 _____

5 _____

6 _____

7 _____

8 _____

9 _____

2 Choose two words that you are finding tricky to spell and write them three times.

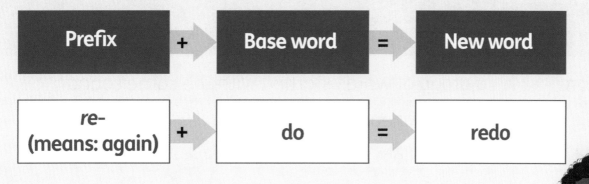

Prefix	+	Base word	=	New word
re- (means: again)	+	do	=	redo

1 Change the meaning of each base word by writing the **re-** prefix before it. Now the meaning of each word includes doing the action again.

tell	
paint	
write	
do	

2 Choose one of the words starting with the **re-** prefix that you wrote. Write it in the box below. Then write a sentence using the word. Look at the example to help you.

Word with prefix	Sentence
retell	I will **retell** the story after I have finished reading the book.

Now try this unit's 'Bringing it together' activity, which your teacher will give you.

GLOSSARY

alliteration	a group of words starting with the same sound
	big black bears
base word	the smallest part of a word that is also a word on its own
	the word 'jump' in 'jumping'
blend	speech sounds that join together in a word
	/st/ is a blend in the word 'stop'
compound word	a new word made out of two words joined together
	sunshine (sun + shine), playground (play + ground)
consonant	a speech sound made by blocking some air with your lips, teeth or tongue
	/b/, /l/, /z/, /v/
consonant digraph	two letters standing for one consonant sound
	sh, ch, th
contraction	two words joined together with some letters missing. An apostrophe shows us where the missing letters are.
	can't (can + not), they're (they + are)
digraph	two letters standing for one phoneme
	sh, ch, oo, ee, ie
diphthong	a kind of long vowel sound that you make by moving your mouth in two ways
	/oi/ in 'boy', /ow/ in 'cow'
homophone	a word that sounds the same as another word but looks different and has a different meaning
	eight, ate

medial	in the middle. A medial phoneme is a speech sound in the middle of a word. This can be a medial vowel or a medial consonant. */o/ is the medial phoneme in the word 'dog'*
onset	the sounds in a syllable before the vowel ***b** stands for the onset in the word 'big'*
phoneme	the smallest speech sound you can hear in a word *the word 'boot' has three phonemes: **/b/**, **long /oo/** and **/t/***
rime	the vowel and other speech sounds at the end of a syllable ***ig** stands for the rime in the word 'big'*
suffix	letters that go at the end of a word to make a new word *the **-s** in 'cats' means 'more than one cat'*
syllable	a part of a word that feels like a beat and has a vowel sound *'weekend' has two syllables (week-end)*
trigraph	three letters standing for one phoneme ***igh** in 'might'*
unvoiced phoneme	a sound made using your breath rather than your voice */**th**/ in 'bath'*
voiced phoneme	a sound made using your voice */**th**/ in 'the'*
vowel	a sound that you voice with your mouth open and not blocked by your lips, teeth or tongue *the **/o/** sound in the word 'dog' is a vowel sound*
vowel digraph	two letters standing for one vowel sound ***ee**, **ay***

When you have finished the activities in each unit, think about how you feel about the work you have completed.

Draw a ✓ if you feel confident using these ideas on your own.

Draw a ✗ if you feel you need to learn more.

Draw a ○ if you are not sure.

Unit	Phonology	Orthography	Morphology
1			
2			
3			
4			
5			
6			
7			
8			
9			
10			
11			
12			
13			
14			
15			
16			
17			
18			
19			
20			
21			
22			
23			
24			
25			
26			
27			
28			

OXFORD UNIVERSITY PRESS